THE CHOCTAW

A TRUE BOOK®
by
Christin Ditchfield

Children's Press®
A Division of Scholastic Inc.

New York Toronto London Auckland Sydney
Mexico City New Delhi Hong Kong
Danbury, Connecticut

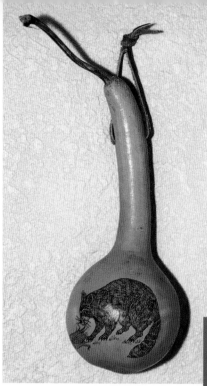

Content Consultant
Liz Sonneborn

*The photograph on the title
page shows a portrait of
Choctaw leader Peter Pitchlynn
(also known as Snapping
Turtle), painted in 1834*

A drinking gourd
decorated with
raccoon art

Library of Congress Cataloging-in-Publication Data
Ditchfield, Christin.
    The Choctaw / by Christin Ditchfield.
        p. cm. — (A true book)
    Includes bibliographical references and index.
    ISBN 0-516-22818-8 (lib. bdg.)   0-516-25589-4 (pbk.)
    1. Choctaw Indians—Juvenile literature. 2. Indians of North America—
Southern States—History—Juvenile literature. I. Title. II. Series.
E99.C8D57 2005
976.004'97387—dc22   2004030919

7 8 9 10 R 14 13 12 11 10
                    62

Contents

THE CHOCTAW TODAY

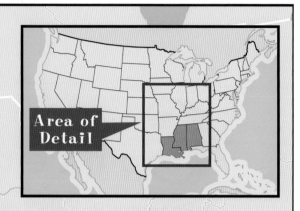

Area of
Detail

KANSAS

MISSOURI

KENTUCKY

OKLAHOMA

ARKANSAS

TENNESSEE

Mississippi R.

MISSISSIPPI

ALABAMA

0   150 miles

0   150 kilometers

LOUISIANA

TEXAS

N
W   E
S

Gulf of Mexico

A Peaceful People

According to an old story, the American Indian tribe known as the Choctaw came from a **sacred** hill. The hill was called *Nanih Waiya*—the mother mound—and was located near what is now Noxapater, Mississippi. Tribe members called themselves *Chata'* or

Chata' Ogla. The Chickasaw nicknamed them the *Pansh Falaia*, or "long hairs." Unlike the men in other southeastern tribes, the Choctaw did not

The Choctaw lived along the Mississippi River.

shave their heads. They wore their hair in long braids.

The Choctaw grew to become the largest tribe in the region. Their territory covered 23 million acres of land in Mississippi, Alabama, and Louisiana. These peace-loving people lived on farms and in villages along the Mississippi River. They could defend themselves if they had to, but they preferred to live in **harmony** with those around them.

He Who Puts Out and Kills was a Choctaw chief in the 1800s. He died in 1838.

The oldest and wisest man in the village became the leader or chief. He taught the younger men how to protect and provide for the tribe. He organized tribal ceremonies

and celebrations. When necessary, he made the decisions
that affected the future of
the tribe.

Choctaw women made all
the decisions for their families. A Choctaw woman was
responsible for taking care of
everyone in her family and
keeping them clothed and
fed. She raised the children
and looked after the elderly.
She was honored as the head
of her home.

Living on the Land

The Choctaw were expert farmers. Their land was perfectly suited for growing crops. It had rich soil and plenty of fresh water, and the weather was good for growing things. Women cleared the fields and planted the crops. They grew corn, beans, sunflowers, squash, and melons. Women also gathered

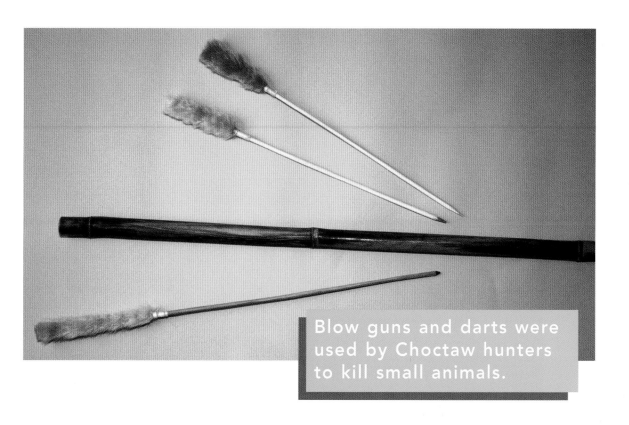

Blow guns and darts were used by Choctaw hunters to kill small animals.

nuts and berries and plants that were safe to eat. They prepared all of the family meals. The men hunted for deer, bear, and turkey. They fished in the rivers, traveling in **dugout** canoes.

Choctaw families lived in homes with thatched roofs like the one on this home.

The Choctaw built circular lodges for their homes. Wooden poles gave the lodges their shape. The roofs were covered with palmetto branches, grass, or cane reeds. Sometimes, the frames of the walls might be filled in with clay and crushed shells; other times, they were wrapped in animal hides or grass mats. There was usually one door, which opened to the south. On cold nights, a family would light a fire in a pit in the center of their lodge. A small opening in the roof allowed the smoke to escape.

In the summer, men wore belts and breechcloths (aprons with front and back flaps hanging from the waist). Women wore short deerskin skirts. In the winter, men and boys wore leggings and long shirts. Women wore longer dresses and deerskin shawls. Both men and women wore soft leather shoes called moccasins. They decorated their bodies by wearing earrings, feathers, face paint, and tattoos.

A Choctaw man wears a collar made of feathers as a decoration.

Ishtaboli

The Choctaw loved to play Ishtaboli—stickball. Using a stick with a pocket at the end, players tried to toss a leather ball down the playing field and into their opponent's goal. Players could not touch the ball with their hands. They had to be skilled with the stick. To keep their opponents from scoring, players could trip, bump, stomp, or tackle them. It was a rough game, and sometimes somebody got hurt. But that didn't spoil the fun!

Competitions were held between teams from different villages, with hundreds of players participating. The men played first, and then the women took the field. Tribe members often bet on the outcome of the games. Medicine men served as coaches, cheering on the team and singing for good luck. Stickball is still a popular game among the Choctaw today.

Living in Harmony

The Choctaw lived in peace and harmony with nature and with one another. Dancing was an important way to celebrate the different events of life. The Choctaw performed the Friendship Dance, the Wedding Dance, and the War Dance. To celebrate the

A group of Choctaw perform the Eagle Dance.

new harvest, they performed
the Green Corn Dance.
Animal dances honored the

various creatures that shared the Choctaw lands. All of these dances were part of religious ceremonies.

The Choctaw loved music. Villages competed with each other to write the best new songs for the next festival. They practiced their songs in secret, keeping an eye out for spies or "song thieves."

The Choctaw were also skilled artists. Women creat- ed beautiful beadwork and pottery. They wove complicated patterns into their attractive swamp-cane baskets.

A Choctaw woman weaves a beautiful basket.

Choctaw healers collected plants and herbs to treat illnesse

The Choctaw did not **worship** any one particular god or spirit. They expressed their devotion to many different spirit beings. They looked for spiritual guidance from **prophets**, rainmakers, medicine men, and healers. In addition to prayer, healers used a variety of herbs and plants to cure disease. They created medicines and treatments for fever, stomach pain, snake bites, pneumonia, arthritis, and other illnesses.

Friends and Enemies

In the 1500s, the Choctaw came into contact with Spanish explorers along the Mississippi River. Sometimes, there was violence between the groups. The Choctaw also got to know the French fur traders, **missionaries**, and **settlers** who followed the explorers.

Spanish explorer Hernando de Soto was the first European to see the Mississippi River.

In the 1700s, European nations often fought for control of the eastern part of North America. The Choctaw sided with France against

This battle was just one of many fought during the French and Indian War. The Choctaw fought on the side of the French during this conflict.

Great Britain in the French and Indian War. France eventually lost control of their territory to Great Britain. During the American Revolution and the

War of 1812, Choctaw warriors helped the Americans defeat the British.

The Choctaw worked to keep the peace between settlers and other southeastern tribes. They knew it was necessary for every-one to learn to work together and live together in peace. The Choctaw became known to white settlers as one of the Five Civilized Tribes, along with the Cherokee, Creek, Chickasaw, and Seminole.

Each spring the Choctaw hold a Trail of Tears Walk to honor their ancestors who were forced to march hundreds of miles to Oklahoma.

women, and children died of starvation and disease along the way. With great courage and determination, those who survived immediately began rebuilding their lives.

The Chocktaw Today

There are more than 65,000 Choctaw in the United States today. Most of them live on reservations in Oklahoma or on tribal lands in Mississippi. There are also smaller communities of Choctaw in Alabama and Louisiana.

The U.S. government recognizes the right of American Indians to govern themselves. The Choctaw Nation of Oklahoma and the Choctaw Nation of Mississippi have their own constitutions. They elect leaders to represent them at tribal councils.

The Choctaw believe that education is very important to the future of the tribe. Since the 1830s, they have organized their own system

The Choctaw work hard to make sure their children receive a good education.

of schools, colleges, and universities to teach the next **generation** and prepare them to be successful in life.

Code Talkers

During World War I (1914–1918), many Choctaw were proud to serve in the U.S. military. One day, an officer heard some of the men speaking in their native language and had an idea. The Germans had cracked the U.S. secret codes for sending messages between commanders and their companies. What if the U.S. military used the Choctaw language as a code?

Within hours, the Choctaw soldiers were assigned to different companies in the area. They were able to transmit top secret U.S. Army information without the Germans figuring out what the messages were. The language was so different from European languages that German code experts could not crack the code.

The Choctaw language was used as a code again during World War II. Other American Indian languages such as Navajo and Comanche were also used. The codes based on these languages were never cracked.

Today, the Choctaw live just like other Americans. They shop in the same stores and buy the same kinds of clothes. They make their homes in houses and apartment buildings. Members of the tribe have many different careers. Some make their living as doctors, nurses, lawyers, or engineers. Others work as farmers or fishers. Some operate businesses such as campgrounds, restaurants, hotels, and tourist attractions.

Choctaw Chief Phillip Martin speaks at the grand opening of a restaurant at a resort in Mississippi that is owned by the tribe.

While they live their modern American lives, the Choctaw also work hard to keep their

A girl studies the Choctaw language with the help of her uncle.

history and **culture** alive. They want their children and grandchildren to grow up proud to be Choctaw. There are newspapers and magazines that help celebrate the Choctaw way of life. Members of the tribe can connect through Web sites and online groups to share their heritage.

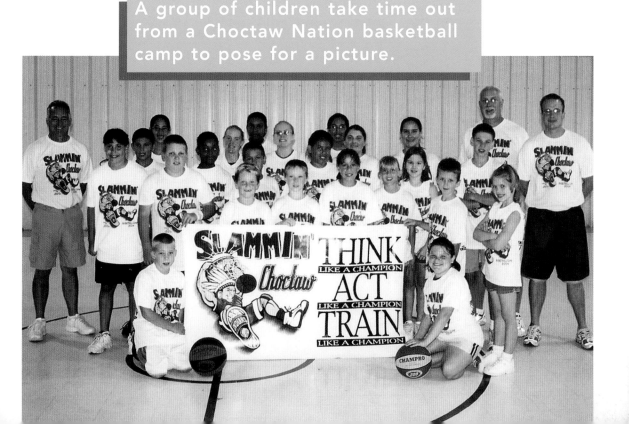

A group of children take time out from a Choctaw Nation basketball camp to pose for a picture.

Museums feature collections of tribal documents, as well as photographs and displays of ancient clothing, pottery, and tools.

Every summer, thousands of people from all over the country gather at the Choctaw Fair in Mississippi and the Annual Choctaw Labor Day Festival in Oklahoma. Tribe members dress in traditional costumes

A Choctaw dancer performs wearing colorful traditional clothing.

A Choctaw woman performs at an outdoor arena in Phoenix. Performances help keep traditional Choctaw arts alive and help teach people about the tribe's culture.

and perform ceremonial songs and dances. Traditional Choctaw arts and crafts are displayed, and delicious recipes are shared. There are rodeos, parades, princess pageants, and, of course, world championship stickball competitions! All of these activities help the Choctaw people celebrate their history and preserve their traditions for future generations.

To Find Out More

Here are some additional resources to help you learn more about the Choctaw:

 **Books**

Harrell, Beatrice Orcutt. **How Thunder and Lightning Came to Be: A Choctaw Legend.** Penguin Putnam Books for Young Readers, 1995.

Koestler-Grack, Rachel A. **The Choctaw: Stickball Players of the South.** Capstone Press, 2003.

Lassieur, Allison. **The Choctaw Nation.** Capstone Press, 2001.

Miller, Jay. **American Indian Families.** Children's Press, 1996.

Miller, Jay. **American Indian Festivals.** Children's Press, 1996.

Sherrow, Victoria. **The Choctaw.** Rourke Publishing Group, 1997.

Organizations and Online Sites

Choctaw Literature

http://www.indigenouspeople. net/choctaw.htm

Visit this site to read traditional Choctaw stories and legends.

Choctaw Nation of Oklahoma

www.choctawnation.com

Visit this official site of the Choctaw Nation of Oklahoma to find out more about the tribe's history and culture. Links to information about events such as the annual Labor Day Festival and powwows are also provided.

Choctaw Vision

www.choctaw.org

Learn more about the Choctaw at this official site of the Mississippi Band of Choctaw Indians. Links to detailed information about the tribe's history and culture are provided. You can also find out more about the band's government and businesses.

Important Words

culture the way of life of a group of people

dugout a canoe made from the outer portion of a log

generation people born around a certain time

harmony calm, free of disturbances

missionary a person who travels to another place to share faith and do good works

prophet a person who predicts what will happen in the future

reservation land set aside by the government as a place for American Indians to live

sacred holy; having to do with religion; something deserving of great respect

settler a person who makes a home in a new place

worship to express love and devotion

Index

Meet the Author

Christin Ditchfield is an author, conference speaker, and host of the nationally syndicated radio program *Take It to Heart!* Her articles have been featured in magazines all over the world. A former elementary school teacher, Christin has written more than thirty books for children on a wide range of topics, including sports, science, and history. She makes her home in Sarasota, Florida.

Photographs © 2005: AP/Wide World Photos: 37 (Rogelio Solis); Art Resource, NY/George Catlin/Smithsonian American Art Museum, Washington, DC, USA: 1, 8, 15, 16, 17, 19; Choctaw Nation: 30 (Lisa Reed), 39 (Vonna Shults); Corbis Images/Buddy Mays: cover, 42, 43; Getty Images: 38 (Shelly Katz/Time Life Pictures), 26 (MPI/Hulton Archive); Library of Congress: 28; Mississippi Band of Choctaw Indians, Tribal Archives: 33; Nativestock.com/Marilyn "Angel" Wynn: 2, 11, 22; North Wind Picture Archives: 6, 12 (Nancy Carter), 25; Peabody Museum of Archaeology and Ethnology, Harvard University: 40 (88-51-10/50694A); Raymond Bial: 21; William Hammond Mathers Museum, Indiana University: 35.

Map by Bob Italiano